Take What You Need Leave the Rest

Take What You Need Leave the Rest

Lauren Milo

Contents

Relationship to Self

1

Are You Meeting Your Needs?

A need is defined as anything that if it were taken away from you, would leave you physically, emotionally or mentally **harmed**. Most people struggle to meet their needs. We spend so much time focusing on others that we neglect taking care of ourselves on a daily basis. I'm not just talking about the basic needs of food, shelter, and water. I'm talking about the added emotional and psychological needs we don't typically address.

Ask yourself - what do you need? Do you need to feel respected by your partner? Do you need to express your creativity daily? Do you need to move your body consistently or be in the sunlight?

Everyone will have a different list but the key here is to identify if and how you're meeting these needs every single day. The other important aspect of this exercise is that **only you can meet your needs**.

Make a list of your needs, check it twice. Ask yourself "if I didn't receive this, would I be hurt?" If the answer is yes - it's a need. Challenge yourself to fulfill it.

2

Do You Need It or Do You Want It?

If you made a list of needs, chances are you had some wants on that list. Wants pretend to be needs a lot of the time. That's why they're sneaky. They trick you into believing that your life would be lesser off if they weren't part of it. As I defined in the *Meeting Your Needs* section, a need is anything that if it were taken away from you, would leave you physically, emotionally or mentally harmed. Thus, if you're not disrupted by the removal of something, it's probably a want.

There's no rhyme or reason when it comes to wants. They're subjective and wholly personal. In order to obtain your wants, meet your needs first. When you don't meet your needs, and try wanting something - things can get confusing. For example, going on a date and wondering the whole time if they like you.

When you meet your needs first and then go after what you want, you can maintain your peace of mind. So on your date, instead of wondering if they like you, you can ask yourself the ultimate question: **"Do I want you in my life?"**

5

It's a lot easier to identify if you want something when you know you don't need it.

3

You Have Everything You Need

In the process of self-growth, you reach a point where you have everything you need inside of you. When you've gotten really good at meeting your needs, you are often presented opportunities to give them up. This shows up as old habits that tempt you or test you. They essentially show up out of the blue and make you begin to doubt your own resolve.

These moments welcome in the potential for insecurity, self-doubt and self-blame. When this occurs you begin to feel out of alignment and will have further difficulty staying in a space of elevated peace of mind.

Remember, you have everything you need inside of you.

If the opportunity presented takes away or reduces one of your needs, think long and hard before engaging with it. For example, if a partner you thought you needed comes out of the blue, ask yourself: "what need were they fulfilling for me?"

If you find that you've been fulfilling that need on your own and you "want" to see them you, by all means make a life choice. If you find that you haven't fulfilled that need and desperately want them to, perhaps pause on the action until you've met your own needs first.

4

Go Where You Need, Before You Go Where You Are Nee

Go where you need before you go where you are needed. It is pivotal to take care of your own needs before you are able to meet the needs of others. So often we think that meeting our own needs is a selfish act. Yet, it is actually a self-less act.

If you're able to meet your own needs, you are prioritizing your mental, emotional and physical well-being. You are ensuring that when you show up for others you are operating at your highest level. As a result, you are able to stay present and focused and exhibit a greater capacity for care.

5

It's Easy to Be Useful

It's easy to be useful. When you're useful, you receive external validation that you are worth something to someone else. When you seek purpose, you are striving to be something for yourself.

In the grand scheme of things, would you rather serve others or serve yourself? If you answered yourself, congratulations. You want a sense of purpose. In order to find it, begin evaluating where you are useful to others. When you have a list of those scenarios, play out what it would mean for you to swap out those acts of usefulness for acts that fulfill you and only you.

The goal is to establish actions that cultivate you feeling good for yourself before you step into a space of being of use to someone else.

6

Root to Rise

Root to rise is the concept of planting yourself in your life so fully that you're able to see opportunities as they come to you. This goes against what we often do when changes occur. We typically look outside of ourselves and search the world and the people around us to determine what to do next. When we step outside of ourselves, we are immediately leaving a space of confidence. This prevents us from being able to see any next step clearly.

When you root down, you plant yourself fully in your own world. You invest in yourself and the things that feed your soul. Rooting involves paying more attention to what serves you in your life and investing time and energy into it.

Rising means releasing your time and energy from the things that do not serve you. This requires a process of acknowledging how they served you in the past and actively choosing to no longer invest in them. In doing so, you intentionally free yourself up. You are inviting more opportunities to your doorstep because you now have the space for them.

Investing in Yourself

We spend so much time investing in others that we forget to invest in ourselves. Investing in yourself takes effort. It requires you to turn inward and evaluate the spaces where you feel you are not operating at your highest capacity. It implies that you are shining a light on things that you would rather ignore.

Take those areas and begin to consider how you want to make them better. This stage of change is totally in your control. Pick and choose the pieces of you that you want to enhance and the pieces you want to leave by the wayside.

When you invest in yourself, you will no longer require other to fulfill you. You will become discerning of who you spend your time with. As you elevate your spirit, take with you those who rise right alongside of you.

8

Put Into Instead of Put On

Focus on the things you want to put into your life instead of what's being put on your life by others. The things that are "put on" are constraints outside sources that limit your potential growth. If you focus on those, you will always feel tight, constricted and stuck.

When focusing on things you want to "put into" your life, you are pushing those constraints off of you. You are intentionally filling yourself up so much with your own thoughtfully chosen items that eventually, there is no more room for an external condition to limit your exponential growth.

Where Do You Treat Yourself Poorly?

Perhaps the most difficult thing to do when you're building up self-confidence is evaluating how and where you treat yourself poorly. It can be overwhelming and scary to pay attention to the situations where you lower your standards or expectations and engage in dynamics that no longer serve you.

If you're on the path to building self-confidence, remember that the path is not a straight shot. It is the ups and downs that come from you building the muscle of self-confidence. You will have wins where you treat yourself phenomenally. You will have losses where you go back to old habits. But in the pursuit of building yourself up, it takes constant practice to become effortless. Never stop trying.

10

Are You Hibernating to Heal?

Isolation. Hiding. Protecting. All interchangeable words when it comes to healing from hurt. The act of removing yourself so fully from a situation that you go deep into self-protection is innate. We learn how to curl into ourselves in order to lick our wounds and rebuild our confidence. But when you have been hibernating too long, healing becomes a hindrance.

There is a very specific spot where you have healed but you feel hesitant to emerge back out into your world. This moment requires you to be courageous. It demands you show up for yourself. At this exact moment, everything in your mind will tell you to stay put and stay "safe" because it's more comfortable to be in your state of hibernation than it is to experience living expansively again.

Remember, growth cannot exist in stagnation so you must find a way to move past hibernation and back out into the wonderful world of air, light and movement. You will know when you've overstayed your welcome in the hibernation phase because you will feel yourself falling down instead of rising up.

11

Control, You Finicky Bitch

Oh man, how often did I try to control things because I didn't trust myself? When I hear someone say they have a need to control I often ask why? What happens if you don't control the person, scenario, the output? There's a slight pause. The questioning glance. The fidget of their hands. The hesitant response of "I don't know."

"I don't know" fits in the space between Controlling Others and Trusting Yourself. When you pull control back from all the external things you want to hold onto, you land in the space of the unknown which is uncomfortable. It's easy to panic and go back to controlling others because the discomfort becomes so great.

Allow the discomfort to pass over you like water. It will not stay with you forever and once it passes you will have gained the slightest ounce of trust in yourself, which is more than you started with. Keep accumulating until you are full.

23

12

Self-Love

To begin the journey of self-love, awareness is a requirement. We have to become aware of all aspects of ourselves, not just the ones we already love. Self-love does not mean we lean so fully into positivity that we ignore or negate the aspects of ourselves we'd rather not address.

Self-love inherently means having an awareness and understanding about those parts and instead of shunning them, embracing them as parts of ourselves that we continue to work on.

Self-love is challenging but it is a beautiful process of holding ourselves accountable for who we are now and who we are actively working to become.

13

Shame Sits at the Bottom of the Barrel

Shame is pervasive. It can become poisonous to your soul and your concept of self when you receive it. It breeds in the darkness of secrecy. You can't heal from shame. You have to get rid of it.

It's common to assume that Shame is produced internally. It may be shocking to consider that **Shame has to be given to you from an outside source.** You can't feel shame about something if you don't have an external reference point. If I left you on an island by yourself, you wouldn't be able to produce the feeling of shame because there would be no one to give it to you.

When talking about shame, I use very specific language. I never use the language "I'm ashamed." I say, "I **feel shame about** something". The subtle difference is critical. If I say "I'm ashamed about something," I am consistently reinforcing that there is a part of my soul that should be kept hidden and locked away because shame is attached to it.

If I say "I feel shame about something," I rip shame's tentacles off of me. I am now able to recognize that I feel shame about something because it was given to me from something outside of myself.

This change in language pushes you to evaluate who or what gave you the shame in the first place. Just because something is given to you, does not mean you have to keep it. You have always maintained the autonomy to give back things that don't suit you or weren't yours to begin with.

The next time you feel shame, use the following exercise:

I feel shame about [insert topic], and it was given to me by [insert person or experience]. Do I want to keep this shame? [yes or no].

If the answer is no: say internally or out loud: I give this shame back to its original source. It's not part of me. If the answer is yes: Keep digging. Pull the thread of shame and you will discover that somewhere along the line, you were given something and you forgot it wasn't yours to begin with.

14

Guilt

G uilt is produced as the result of an internal conflict between you and yourself. When you fight with yourself, it's often because you have a concept of what feels right and good for you, and then you choose to go against that. It's normal - we are people with free will and no obligation to always choose the most ideal thing. When we choose to actively go against our higher self, the resulting feeling is guilt.

Guilt doesn't mean you've done something wrong. It is simply the result of having an awareness that there was an alternative option to what you chose to do that may have resulted in a more positive outcome.

Resolving Guilt and Shame

You approach resolving guilt and shame in different ways. With shame, you eradicate it. You identify where you received it from and actively choose to no longer accept it. With guilt, you have to go back to the moment you disappointed yourself. Get curious about why you chose to take an action. This isn't about self-blame. It's about recognizing the factors and conditions that went into leading you to a choice you feel guilty about. When you recognize those conditions, you gain understanding and have awareness for future scenarios that may trigger those sensations again.

Protection vs Defensiveness

Protect and defend are two sides of the same coin when it comes to a sense of self. We confuse protection and defensiveness because they feel similar. Protection guards your heart. Defense keeps others away from it.

The difference between these two concepts is which was you turn. Guarding turns inwards. It's an intentional act that protects something of importance. Defense turns outwards. It's a foolish game of trying to block out the "what ifs" that haven't shown up yet.

In protection, you're able to see opportunities and challenges as they approach you. When you're in a defensive mode, you've left your space of self and have gone out in the anticipation of something going wrong. The moment you leave yourself you are unable to see what is approaching and you fall into the mindset of fighting every battle without asking if it's meant for you in the first place.

17

The Art of Making Yourself Small

There are plenty of moments in life that push us into being smaller versions of ourselves. There are plenty of external conditions and people that bully us into being small. They push us into being lesser versions of ourselves.

But self-deprecation is unique because it is the art of making yourself small when you've not been asked to. It is us against ourselves. It's an internal conflict that begs the question: why do we do it?

When you self-deprecate you constantly reinforce the message that you are in fact not worth being celebrated. Your accomplishments and successes are worth less than others. Over time you internalize that message to such a degree that you begin to believe it as always true.

Pay attention to how, where and why you self-deprecate. Get curious about yourself and begin to contemplate an alternative to putting yourself down. Self-deprecation has never suited you at all, it is time to let it go.

35

18

Throw Away Phrase

Do you find yourself using throw away phrases? Everyone has one. Mine are "it's fine" or "I'm just tired." If you hear me say that, you know that I've given up on trying to advocate for myself.

When I hear clients use throw away phrases, they're often surprised at how many times they use it to dismiss their own needs.

That's what a throw away phrase does. It makes you smaller, it makes you less. If you're going to use a throw away phrase, know why you're doing it. Begin to raise your awareness of the situations or people that make you feel like you need to shrink to fit in.

Some examples of throw away phrases include the following:

"It's fine."
"Whatever."
"It doesn't matter."
"It makes sense"
"I'll just do it."
"It's not a big deal."

When you use one of these, you put a limit on how authentically you can show up. Be mindful of when you limit yourself, you may be doing it more than you think.

37

19

Avoiding Advocating for Yourself?

Advocating for yourself is hard work. It's not something that comes naturally. In fact, it's something that often we only think to do after the fact. But to advocate for yourself is one of the greatest gifts you can give to your soul. You are telling yourself you are worth it, you are worthy and you are deserving of what you seek.

When we avoid advocating for ourselves, we send a message to our soul that we're not worthy of operating at our highest level. We are essentially procrastinating. We prevent ourselves from becoming a better version of us because it will certainly inconvenience others.

You have always been meant to live a bright, expansive life. Of course that will ruffle a few feathers. But would you rather keep the peace and shut your soul in a box or fight for this one glorious life you've been given?

20

What Do You Accept and Reject?

In the early parts of a healing cycle I often ask clients to identify if something was theirs originally or if it was given to them. If they identify a label, a feeling, even a habit as being given to them, I then inquire if they want to continue accepting it as their own or reject it.

Nine times out of ten, they reject it.

Acceptance and rejection are a great tools to establish a sense of self when you're navigating the unfamiliar territory of getting to know you again. They help provide clear boundaries as to what you inherited and what was yours to begin with. I use this exercise when evaluating what labels I've been given since childhood, what stereotypes I carry about myself in relationships and what choices I make so routinely that I fail to ask if they even serve me anymore.

21

Return to Sender

In the second iteration of healing, I replace acceptance and rejection with "Return to Sender." This occurs after you've determined what you've been given by others (often parents). It is a step you take to talk with them and acknowledge that although you've absorbed a lot of what they put on you, you no longer want to shoulder the burden.

You begin by acknowledging with them what you received over the years and then setting a boundary to cease accepting their stuff any further.

For example, if you were talking to parent: "As I was growing up, I felt like you were really hard on me. You shared you had a difficult relationship with your parents and I imagine you must be hurting a lot to have experienced that." [validation]. "But I am trying to grow and I would like to not continue that type of dynamic between you and I. In the future, I'd like to work on a new version of our relationship, one that doesn't put me in a position where I feel pressured by you." [return of information].

Return to sender is similar to making amends in the sense that you are taking ownership of all pieces of your life. The reason return to sender is important, is because it sets a clear and firm boundary

43

that despite years of experiencing something, you are choosing to no longer engage.

22

Your Mom Gives You A Sweater

As you grow up, people hand you labels all day long. From the aunt that tells you that you're "so sensitive" to the friend that tells other people you're the "smart" one in the group - you are constantly absorbing things that other people are telling you about yourself. You're also absorbing their silent expectations.

I invite you to consider this: Your mom gives you a sweater and it's a thoughtful gift. The sweater is kind of your size, it only itches slightly and every once and a while you take it out of your drawer and wear it.

Yet, it never quite fits right and it leaves you with a mild neck rash. But it was given to you by someone you love so every time you take it off, you sigh, think about donating it but inevitably put it back in your drawer. Whenever you see mom, you wear it and it brings her so much joy that you can't bring yourself to ever give it away. But each time it goes back in the drawer, a little part of your soul dies.

Not to state the obvious, but the sweater in this metaphor is the label you passive accepted. When you first receive it, you accept it be-

45

cause it's easy. Over time, you begin to believe the label makes you who you are.

But did you ever stop to ask if your label is even accurate?

Start paying attention to the labels you receive throughout the day. Whether it's a compliment, an insult or a passing comment ask yourself: Do I accept or reject this label?

If you reject it, replace it with a word that better suits you.

If you accept it, think long and hard about the word choice. For example, being labeled "smart" can be positive. So you may be inclined to accept it right off the bat. But what if you resonate with the word intellectual or bright instead? Choose your labels carefully, they're difficult to get rid of and they certainly leave a mark.

23

Fear and Doubt

We often think we are afraid to try something new. We create these narratives that it is fear that's holding us back from the exciting opportunity or taking the leap. What if we've been using the wrong language the entire time? What if it's not fear of something new. But doubt masquerading as fear?

When we use the word fear, everything goes into a fear response. You're never going to feel comfortable making a decision if you keep saying "I'm afraid." Your body tenses up and your mind looks for ways to feel safe. This is exactly why you can overstay your welcome in the comfort zone.

Fear and doubt sit in two totally different areas of the body. Fear is neck down. Doubt is neck up. Fear is neck down because the only one of the senses you have there is feeling/touch. You **feel** fear. In the neck up region of doubt, you have hearing and seeing. Conveniently, these are the two senses that invite others words or actions into your zone of awareness thus you **think** doubt.

When you're about to make a decision think about where it sits in your body. If your stomach drops, you tense up and you feel it. Chances are, it's fear. If you find that it's in the neck up zone, your

47

thoughts are racing and your mind is running in circles, chances are it's doubt.

I invite you to replace "I'm afraid" with "I'm doubtful" the next time you hesitate to choose a new opportunity or you wonder why you haven't taken a leap. Have the courage to get curious about your doubts. Ask why relentlessly until you have gotten to the bottom of it. Once you have, you'll often find that doubts are a lot less scary than fear can ever be.

24

Are You Holding Your Own Fear?

Today I asked someone what they were afraid of. They only listed two things. When I asked what they thought they were afraid of, they listed over ten.

The ten things they listed were all fears that weren't theirs. They were the fears of others. They were holding so much space for other people's fears, doubt and insecurities that over time they began to believe it was their own.

A funny thing happens when you ask yourself what you're really afraid of: you realize it's not very much at all.

25

Insecurity

Insecurity points to a part of yourself you've not yet made your peace with. That's okay! It doesn't mean there's anything wrong with you. It means that there is a part of you that has yet to grow and frankly, you have no obligation to touch it until you're ready.

When we view insecurity through a fear mindset, it suddenly becomes something big, scary, and untouchable. We have learned that insecurities make us weak and open to threat.

What if we changed the narrative? Imagine if identifying your insecurities was an act of strength? How courageous you must be to own all the parts of yourself – even the parts you'd rather forget. If you know what you're insecure about, it makes it that much harder to be used against you. Never let someone use your insecurities as a weapon. Neutralize them by having the courage to face yourself before they expose you.

26

In Spite Of

To do something in spite of contradicts the "fuck it" attitude. When you say fuck it, you could negate or ignore your own feelings around a circumstance. The ignoring is all fine and dandy until it comes back to bite you when the bravado has worn off and you're left wondering "what did I just do?"

Try out doing things "in spite of." Try to go on a date, in spite of the fact you hate dating. Try to mend the relationship with you and friend in spite of the fact that you still carry anger. To act in spite of looks fear directly in the eye and says "Today, I prevent you from winning" and that is a glorious way to live.

27

Apathy: The Path of Least Resistance

The path of least resistance is paved with apathy. Apathy is an obstacle emotion. I know that is counter intuitive to it being a paving stone on the path of least resistance but hear me out. Apathy is an obstacle emotion because it is the obstacle you have to get through in order to move into deeper emotional territory. The reason it's a paving stone is because we often stop right at the obstacle and never conquer it. It's far easier to become apathetic than it is to face some of the stronger emotions.

If you've become apathetic to a situation, ask yourself what emotion sits just below apathy. Is it anger, fear, or worry? Challenge the nature of avoidance to embrace what comes when you switch out apathy for something else. Remember apathy prevents you from feeling. If you can't feel, you can't heal.

28

Are You Enduring or Learning?

How often do we sit through something and experience no joy, no growth, no sensation of change? The spirit of endurance runs strong through much of what we do in our day to day if we're not mindful of encouraging ourselves to learn.

When you feel uninspired, bored or uninterested ask yourself what you are enduring. Then ask yourself when was the last time you were learning in the same area. If it's been awhile, perhaps it's time to open yourself up to learning something new. Endurance in the healing journey can thwart growth. Replace it with encouragement and watch yourself thrive.

29

Cultivating Talent

There is an assumption that if we possess a talent we must use it. Suddenly, a talent takes on a weight of responsibility. We desperately try to confine, shape and reform what is natural, gifted and expansive into something that makes sense to the larger world but may not fit us anymore.

When you spend years trying to make your talent useful to others, you miss out on the opportunity to live in a space of unconditional acceptance and cultivation.

Cultivating a talent is different from utilizing one. When you cultivate, you're fueling future you. It's a thoughtful practice of active choice where you choose to replenish your own soul before serving others. You make thoughtful decisions about how to grow your talent in a way that resonates with you first and foremost. When you're utilizing, you're fueling a circumstance and run the risk of emptying yourself out so much you lose sight of the gifts you began with. Cultivate a garden and it grows. Utilize a garden and it will wither within a season.

30

Seeking Clarity

If you are seeking clarity, go to where you feel clear-headed. You cannot seek clarity in a space that makes you feel trapped, small, or cramped. Go to a space where you feel expansive, free and light. You will find that it's easier to feel clear-headed when the space you are in is clear as well.

31

Flow With the Current

To be in flow with the current of life means that you take life as it comes and you challenge you and only you to become expansive. Flowing with the current of life takes little to no effort because it doesn't engage anyone but yourself. You hold yourself accountable for what you want to accomplish. You challenge yourself to go after the dreams you hold. You embrace the possibility of living a life meant for you as opposed to one assigned to you.

Flowing with the current is a space of self-trust, self-belief and ultimately, self-love. You stay in such a space of self that you rarely, if ever, step outside to change for others. When you are in flow, opportunities show up on your doorstep and you maintain the ability to evaluate if and how they serve you.

32

Leave Nothing Behind

You have everything in front of you. You've left nothing behind. When you think backwards, you move backwards into smaller, tighter spaces that no longer serve you. If you feel tugged backwards, ask yourself what, if anything, you've left there. Recall why you left it behind in the first place. Once you have that awareness, look ahead. Ahead is expansive, ahead is growth. Ahead is a stronger version of you.

Friendships and How You Relate to Others

33

Accommodation

Accommodation is making more room for others by putting up with their words or actions, which leaves less room for you. You accommodate people you love and care about because they show up for you in other ways. But accommodation is equally as detrimental to the soul as tolerance. In both scenarios, you make yourself smaller. Over time, you ask for less or make yourself less. You say less, do less, act less.

If this sounds familiar, it's because it is familiar. It's become acceptable to treat ourselves poorly as long as we treat others better. Think of the amount of times you brush off the fact that your friend is always, without fail fifteen minutes late to dinner. If they're a good friend to you in a myriad of other ways, perhaps the fifteen minutes is no big deal. You accommodate their behavior because they show up for you in ways that are meaningful.

But say this friend actually doesn't show up for you in other ways. You go out and they're always late. They fail to show up for big moments in your life or even to reach out for small check ins. Every time they do, you tamp down your frustration, you say "it's fine" (throw away phrase) and you accommodate it.

69

Brushing off their actions each time with "it's fine" sends a signal to your soul that their time is more valuable than yours. Is that really the message you want to be giving to yourself on a daily basis?

Look for where you accommodate. Ask yourself why. If you don't have a good reason, perhaps it's time to show up more fully as yourself as opposed to making yourself less to accommodate others more.

34

Tolerance and the Act of Putting Up with Things

I define tolerance as "putting up with something and you really don't want to be." It can show up in very clear ways such as "I won't tolerate being treated this way." But it can also show up subtly. For example, I tolerate friends I don't like for the larger good of the friend group or I tolerate the way people treat me because I don't want to rock the boat.

Fear, self-doubt and tolerance go hand in hand. If you're afraid of rocking a boat because you doubt your relationships, you're going to tolerate dynamics that don't serve you and make it harder for you to meet your needs.

How easy do you think it is to meet your need of being heard and seen when you're tolerating less than stellar treatment from friends?

The act of tolerating something invites in an opportunity for you to negate your own needs. From there, it's a slippery slope. Look for areas in your life where you're tolerating (or accommodating) treatment from others. Once you find one area, look for the pattern. Chances are, if you may be neglecting a need which led you to tolerance in the first place.

Friendships Built like Tiramisu

Making a tiramisu requires patience and attention to each layer's quality. Much like tiramisu, building friendships require the same amount of focus and attention. When building and maintaining friendships strive for the three layer approach.

Layer one, the cookie layer: Your sturdy, stable, true and tried friends who share baseline similarities of friendship values. These are typically those who have been with you the longest but you may not see often anymore. Regardless of time or distance, they show up when you need them.

Layer two, the mascarpone cream: Your fun and floaty friends who are there for a good time not a long time. These are your activity specific friends who you can call up and they'll be down for anything.

Layer three, the chocolate powder or shavings (you do you): These friends are those sparks of joy that you encounter on a rare occasion a few times a year. They add a decadent addition to any environment. They often leave you wanting more time with them.

36

Who Do You Orient Yourself To?

Who do you orient yourself to?

When asking yourself this question, consider what you receive from others. What parts of you do they reflect back when you interact? What pieces of your soul shine brighter because of how they support, care and ground you? Do you show up more authentically when they are around?

Surround yourself with people who only bring you closer to yourself. An energizing soul will let you shine as you're meant to. They will not manipulate you into what they want. If you feel off balance or off course around someone, you may be orienting yourself to the wrong person.

37

Comparing Yourself to Others

Comparison to others thwarts feeling capable in yourself. It's not easy to avoid, but when you compare yourself to someone else you are sending a subconscious message to your own soul that another person is worth more than you. You are internalizing that others are above you, hold power over you, and are more valuable than you. You are also shining a brighter light on them with all the attention and energy you provide.

38

Intimidation or Admiration

Intimidation and admiration fall on the same spectrum of aligning yourself with others with one distinct difference: intimidation is the act of looking down on one-self, admiration is the act of looking up to others.

39

Making Sense for Others

So often we find ourselves orienting our decisions, our choices and our mindsets to align with someone else's. We desperately pour ourselves out in an effort to feel seen and heard by those around us. Especially those who tend to question who we are and how we exist.

Instead of continuing to feed into this narrative of emptying ourselves to fulfill another, try using the lens of "making sense."

When someone questions your life choices, ask yourself "what part of my life are they trying to make sense of?" The goal is not to justify their actions but more to become curious about where they are coming from. This can ease the anger, tension and frustration you feel when you receive feedback about your life you didn't ask for.

For example, the aunt who questions why you start work at 10 am may be trying to make sense of why she could never do that. The father who questions if you are "really working" when you work from home may be mourning that he never had that opportunity.

Your life never warrants an explanation to others. When you get curious about where others lead from you're able to subtly push back on those who criticize you and force them to evaluate themselves.

When you cease comparing yourself to others, you automatically enhance your own light. You are gifted and talented and bright and magnetic. You have always been meant to shine upwards and outwards. You have never been meant to be someone else's spotlight.

40

Hold Onto Those Who Hold Onto You

It's easy to be distracted by new, exciting friendships that leave you breathless with excitement. When new people enter your life it becomes almost routine for us to forge quick connections and marvel at how easy it was to build rapport. We can then tend to neglect those who have shown up for us over and over again.

Hold onto those who have held onto you throughout the years. They've provided a sturdy foundation for you to evaluate how you trust others. Recognize your established friendships for what they are: The benchmark for how you measure new individuals and if they are worthy of being in your life.

83

41

Left Behind in Friendships

When we are left behind in friendships where there hasn't been a rupture, it can often be disarming to consider that we have been left behind for no logical reason.

It may be that someone has chosen to move on because they have decided to invest time and energy elsewhere. This does not mean there's anything wrong with you. It simply means they've redirected their attention to prioritize someone or something else. Instead of wasting your precious time and energy trying to convince them to come back, turn towards those who are already prioritizing you instead.

42

Show and Tell

How often do we feel we're putting on a mask to perform for others? It's a brilliant protective technique. If we only show others what we want, they cannot possibly hurt us. But perhaps, instead of performing (which is a one way street) we can learn how to engage in Show and Tell.

In this instance, meeting and engaging with others become a beautiful dance of information back and forth. You learn how to show pieces of yourself in small doses in direct response to what's being told to you. In Show and Tell, you're in a state of control and curiosity as opposed to only control. The transactional nature of show and tell invites others to get to know you but keeps you in a space of comfortable groundedness.

43

Emotional Tornados

Emotional tornados are a term I like to apply to those in your circle who spin into your life and spin out leaving nothing but destruction in their wake. Emotional tornados can occur at any point in life but it's often when we become most insecure that we are at risk of becoming one ourselves.

To move out of the state of being an emotional tornado, we are required to take responsibility for our previous actions. This takes courage but is well worth your time especially if you're focused on healing.

Going back and making amends with those we have brought into our chaotic orbit frees you from carrying emotions and relationships that you have outgrown. It alleviates anxiety you may feel about the situations you engaged in and it calls your attention back to the present which is focused on growth and forward motion.

Romantic Relationships

44

Words and Actions

When you're building a romantic relationship, words and actions must go hand in hand. It's easy to fall into the trap of welcoming in potential relationships that only fulfill one aspect of the word/action requirement because it's easier to focus on the good than the bad.

For instance, a man who does a ton of talking when you see him out but never follows up with scheduling a date. Yet you pitch him to your friends as someone who is *highly invested* in getting to know you. Alternatively, someone who is all about action and hooking up but fails to text you the next day. You justify his lack of text with *he's just busy* and ignore that you only hear from him after 11 pm on a weeknight.

It's easy to convince ourselves that potential partners are meeting the word + action requirement. But when we ignore the glaring gap in our logic, we run the risk of getting into broken heart territory.

If you are in a space where you have one but not both of the word + action scenario, challenge your potential partner to fulfill the second half of the bargain. If they are texting you for a booty call, ask them to dinner. They may say, hey absolutely or ghost you forever.

Either way, you will quickly find out if they are ready, willing and able to be the partner of your dreams or someone not worth your time.

45

Attunement at the Highest Vibration

If you are looking for someone to meet your expectations, you may experience a sense of guilt or pressure. It may feel like you're asking for too much and in turn, you may lower your expectations to accommodate potential partners. You learn how to ask for less and in turn, will receive less.

Instead of seeking a partner that is trying to meet your expectations, look for someone who is attuned to you. Attunement means this partner operates at the same high frequency as you and thus, you will never be required to lower yourself to their level.

Someone attuned to you will show care for who you are and how you operate. They will pay attention to the things that make you happy but also maintain a sense of self that is wholly independent from you. An attuned partner does not need you in their life but instead wants you to be a part of it and they will take great care in ensuring your well-being without sacrificing who they are as a person.

46

The Canoe Metaphor for Partnership

The easiest way to determine you're with the right partner is to think of your relationship like being in a canoe. Picture yourself rowing with your partner with one person in front and one behind.

As you go through life, your positions in the boat will switch. The person in front who was once the priority may be shifted into the second seat of stability. No matter how many times you switch roles, always make sure both you are rowing.

You never want to be in the canoe with a partner that isn't rowing at all.

47

I'm Not Enough For You - Said Everyone, Always

We are conditioned to believe that if someone says "I won't be enough for you," we simply need to expect less. We try harder to make ourselves smaller and begin to accommodate their needs before our own.

When someone says they are not enough for us, what they are really saying is they're unwilling to put in the effort to rise to our standards. They are not going to try to participate in the life and expectations we have set.

If someone says they're not enough for you, take them at their word. They will never be enough for you and you deserve someone who strives to meet you at your highest level.

48

Ask for the Treatment You Require

Asking for better treatment from a partner requires an immense amount of courage because you are putting yourself first. It can also be challenging to ask for better treatment when we've been in cycles of accepting what we're given as opposed to asking for what we need.

If you're in a dynamic that you feel doesn't serve you, begin by evaluating what you require and then asking for what you need. If the person you're interacting with can meet your new standard: amazing! If they cannot, trust that they have shown you what they are capable of and consider what it would mean for you to find someone who can.

49

I Will Try Harder

So often we think if we just try enough the partner who left us will come back. We are conditioned to believe that there is something wrong with us if they don't.

What if the reason they haven't come back is not because you were not enough for them but because they don't care? Not that they don't care about you but rather that they don't care about investing time or energy into your mutual dynamic because they lazy and uninterested. Perhaps we should stop trying to be enough for someone who can't be bothered. We should stop beating ourselves up for not being able to keep someone who didn't want to be kept in the first place.

Instead let us try to be enough for ourselves and only then, let us seek to find a partner that shows the utmost care for who we have become.

50

Unwanted Does Not Mean Unworthy

How often does being unwanted by someone make us feel like we are worthless or worth-less than others? Being unwanted by someone does not mean something is wrong with you. It simply means your purposes and intentions don't align. You each hold different expectations for what you seek from one another.

When expectations don't align, even if you got what you wanted – you would not feel fulfilled.

Feeling unwanted hurts like hell. But it does not mean that any piece of you is worth less than someone else. Do not beat yourself up for not being someone's cup of tea. There is someone out there in the world looking for your exact flavor. Have the patience and stamina to wait it out.

51

Perpetuating the Hurt of Others

After we have been hurt by someone especially during a break up, there is the initial period of grieving. Within that time, comes anger, sadness and perhaps even resentment. When that period wears off, it's typical to continue engaging in the hurt because we've become so familiar with it, so comfortable in its presence that it feels scary to let it go.

Why do we continue to hurt after we've been hurt? Because we enjoy the badge of honor that comes with pain and neglect to consider what we are missing out on in the joyful parts of our lives.

Pay attention to how and when you continue to engage in hurt that's already past it's grieving period. If you're continuing it, ask yourself what purpose does this serve? Remember, in this phase, you are the only one hurting yourself.

Transitions

52

Fear-Based Decision Making

The fear-based decision model is perhaps no more prevalent than when we are in college. College has prescribed rules and regulations to follow in order to succeed. However, these rules and regulations are steeped in the threat of failure. The mere thought of making the wrong choice or failing to fulfill a regulation can lead to a full blown anxiety spiral. And the thing is, it's not your fault that this happens.

The college academic system uses fear as a motivator. It's meant to inspire you to make choices but it actually conditions you to internalizing more and more fear until it becomes unbearable. It's no surprise then that when you graduate and you carry an unhealthy amount of fear about your future, that most of us crack under the pressure.

We become indecisive and paralyzed by the fear that we may make the wrong decision and our lives will be ruined.

Moving out a fear-based decision making model requires effort and focus. In order to do so, begin by paying attention to your body's response to decisions. A decision that is right for you will feel calm and gentle. A decision that's not meant for you will feel tense, keyed up and leave you restless. If you stay in a space of calm, you will always make the right call.

53

Graduating College

Graduating college is a time fraught with indecision. When you've spent four years making fear-based decisions it can be challenging to start approaching choices from a space of confidence and self-trust.

It is easy to begin questioning the choices that you make over those four years because you're constantly seeking and receiving feedback from others about how they view your choices. They may question your decision making skills and over time, it's no surprise you begin to lose your sense of self.

You have always known who you are. Quiet the noise around you and go back to the things that feel right. Not the things that "make the most sense" in others eyes. When you do so, you can begin to build a life worth living for you and only you.

54

Managing Yourself After College

Learning how to manage yourself is a tricky task because it requires you to be in tune with your own needs. If you've recently graduated college, you aren't quite adept at meeting your own needs because you may not even know what they are.

In order to identify your needs, pay attention to how you feel every moment of every day. It sounds simple and childish, but holding awareness for how you take care of your physical, emotional and mental well-being can mean the difference between living an authentic life and living a life for others.

When learning how to manage yourself, strive for equilibrium. If you're at the extreme ends of the spectrum in any of the three groups, figure out a way to bring yourself back into balance.

If and when it feels as though you don't know where to go or what to do, choose one thing to ground yourself to. Whether this be a city, a job, a salary amount or a home: pick one and commit to it. Every other piece of the puzzle will soon fall into place.

55

Get Back to You

Periods of transition are scary because we begin to doubt our own ability to make choices. We become so unsure of what feels right for us that we often choose things out of fear as opposed to assuredness. If this is occurring, stop where you are. Go back to the things that you love, the things that make you feel most like you. Of course I'm sure you're saying 'I have no idea what those things are." If that is the case, rewind back to your favorite childhood activities and give them a try.

You're not aiming for perfection. You're aiming to illicit the sensation of familiarity in your soul. When you do that enough times, you will begin to reacquaint yourself with who you have always been and future decision making will become easier.

With every decision that pops up, the only thing you have to ask is: "Does this make me feel like myself?"

56

Make a Name for Yourself

We use this phrase post-college all the time. We implore college graduates to "make a name for themselves." As though, who they are now, is not possibly enough. We imply they haven't learned or garnered enough skills to succeed in the "real world." We hand them fear, shame, and self-doubt along with their diplomas and what for?

Perhaps we should try handing them encouragement to live life authentically. If we choose to celebrate the curiosity, exploration and identity-building that comes from that phase of life we have the opportunity to produce a new generation of people who do not fear who they are born as and instead embrace their livelihood.

57

Anxiety About the Job Hunt

The reason the job hunt elicits such an identity crisis is because we may have never been thoughtful about choosing *the right job for us* in the first place. We may have chosen our jobs to fulfill other people's expectations or followed what we were told to do because it "makes the most sense" in others eyes.

If you're unsure of who you are and what job is right for you, look at the advice you've received. Ask yourself if you are passively accepting it. This means that you take others advice and automatically believe it to be true for you. Challenge yourself to review the advice again and then decide if what they say is actually applicable and beneficial to you.

Remember, no one on this earth knows you better than you know yourself. Each time you review advice you've passively accepted, you're moving towards a space where you will no longer seek other's wisdom for your life choices because you already know your way.

58

Receiving Feedback

Receiving feedback or criticism can leave us breathless. It's the shock of someone telling us that something is wrong and we often take it to mean that something is wrong with us as a person.

But feedback about a situation does not necessarily mean something is wrong. Feedback can be given as a means for drawing your awareness to an area that may prevent you from moving upward in growth.

When you receive feedback first ask yourself "do I accept it to be true or reject it as false?" If you accept it, look for actionable steps towards growth. If you reject it, inquire as to why it was given in the first place. You may find that the feedback you received was really never meant for you at all.

59

Failure Means You Tried

When you learn to walk, you learn to fall. The inherent act of learning something new ties to the given that inevitably, you will stumble and fall or fail.

Failure receives a negative connotation because we view it through the lens that failure means something is wrong with us.

If we fail, it means we tried. If we tried, it means we're building resiliency. If we build resiliency, it means we always have our own back and what more could you want from yourself than to always hold onto you?

60

Whose Expectations Are You Living For?

One day we wake up and realize the life we've been living doesn't quite fit us anymore. We may find that we are uncomfortable in one or multiple areas of our life including our job, the city we live in and maybe even the partner we chose.

If you're in this space, the only question you need to ask is, "Whose expectations am I living for?"

Think about your past decisions and see who you were trying to please. Was it yourself or others? Others can mean partners, friends, larger society etc. The important thing is that you begin identifying who you were trying to please and then begin attempting to only please yourself. At first, this will be clunky and awkward. It may even feel scary and off balance. But with effort and time, you will begin to build your own foundation. You may even recognize that your own expectations, the high ones you held yourself too, actually need to be amended because they were external recognition as opposed to internal growth.

61

When You've Lost a Piece of Yourself

During the difficult times where you can't remember who you are or where you went, it's normal to begin searching in the world for the pieces of you that have gone missing. In these times, the last thing you want to do is search the globe.

Your mind and body have the unique gift of protection. During times of distress and fear, they put the best parts of you away for safe-keeping until it's safe to come back out.

You won't find yourself in someone else. It won't matter how far and wide you go because the pieces of you that you've been looking for, have been inside you all along. You just put yourself away until later.